MARBLE DUST

Gary Metras

Červená Barva Press
Somerville, Massachusetts

Červená Barva Press
P.O. Box 440357
W. Somerville, MA 02144

www.cervenabarvapress.com

Bookstore: www.thelostbookshelf.com

Production: Allison O'Keefe

Cover photo: "Ionic column capital, 4th-5th century BCE, the Acropolis, Athens. Photo by the author."

ISBN: 978-1-950063-95-6

Library of Congress Control Number: 2023951995

ALSO BY GARY METRAS

Roses in Lyric Light: Love Poems
A Room Full of Walls
The Yearnings
The Necessities
The Night Watches
Destiny's Calendar
The Adastra Reader (Editor)
Center of the Spiral
Northampton Poem
Seven Stones for Seven Poems
Seagull Beach
Today's Lesson
Until There Is Nothing Left
Greatest Hits 1980-2006
Francis d' Assisi 2008
Two Bloods: Fly Fishing Poems
The Moon in the Pool
White Storm
Captive in the Here
River Voice
River Voice II
Vanishing Points

CONTENTS

I.

Marble Dust   3
Making Love in Athens   4
The Room of Faces   5
Paola   6
#4729 Silver Diadem with Dentilated Border   7
After the Revelation   9
The Butcher   10
The Flesh in Marble   11
How the Conquerors Settled   15
Peace   16
The Anonymous Closet   17
Beneath the Blue Realm   18
Smyrna   19
Belly Dancer   21
Briseis in Midtown   22
Stealing Troy   23

II.

A Kiss Behind The Campidoglio   31
Villa Pomphili Park   32
History as Hobby   34
In the Sistine Chapel   36
The Colosseum   40
In Three Languages   41
Outside the Keats-Shelley House   43
Saint Matthew in the Stone   44
Ruins   45
Leonardo   48
Juliet on the Balcony   51
The Bridge of Sighs   52
One Day in the Apennines   53

III.

Francis d'Assisi 2008   57

IV.

A Paris Christmas   79
The Beautiful Language   80
Gravity Likes You Going Down   81
Oberammergau   83
Swimming with the Swans   84
Cable Car Ride   86
The Economics of Rain   87
Beethoven in the Rain   88
The Day Before Her 50th Birthday   93
A Full Moon in Switzerland   94
Age 23 Wordsworth Sleeps in Stonehenge   95
Emerson at Grasmere   96
Oscar Wilde Brings Flowers To His Wife's Grave   97
Another Miracle in the English Channel   98
Daughter of Alexandria   99
When I Saw the Wild Rabbit   101
Born in Water   102

For Natalie

MARBLE DUST

I.

MARBLE DUST

These are the shoes I wore
to walk the Acropolis in Athens.

I propped a foot on
the Parthenon's step to place

my eyes within the cold glow of marble
to better trace the column's curve

up to the pediment and the cobalt sky
beyond, empty of clouds, of gods.

Empires and deities come and gone.
All those orations, the pledges,

the routine, the grandiose,
evaporated, circling, invisible, above us.

Men and marble. One temporary.
One a truth revealed.

Plato and Phidias, Pericles and Archimedes, all dust
that I carry, lovingly, on these shoes.

MAKING LOVE IN ATHENS

The wife from the café in the alley beneath
our room at Hotel Acropol
is shouting at her husband again.
Here, where they made lust divine
and worshipped the body, she begins each day arguing.
Perhaps it is strictly business—
receipts low, floor unswept, the hired help
who drinks? Last night
when we sat on the wobbly chairs on the cobbled walk
to order tea and share dessert,
she nodded and smiled from behind the bar.
Is it darkness that calms her the way
it did Clytemnestra?
Maybe her husband, short and balding,
looks too long at the young women
so free with their boyfriends, chatting and eating,
their eyes lowered beneath the moon's rising?
Here, where cities and dynasties have crumbled
because of love, we lie listening to our pulses quieting
as the woman's anger ignites.
We could shut the window and live just within ourselves
as Persephone learned to do,
but we know a few minutes more will subside her ire
and then the only sound will be
starched sheets wrinkling.

THE ROOM OF FACES

A room in an Athens' museum is all heads
on pedestals, a maze of gods and mortals,
their marble hair like solid water, chins

clean or plaited beards, mouths caught
in oration, or the stern calm of leadership.
For some the noses are smashed, the lips

cracked as valleys after earthquake. Along
the walls shelves of heads broken, oddly angled
as if they doubted the hearts of all who pass

seeming so intact. And in the eyes of each one
a lost story, a forgotten message. Someone
is saying, "In the cellar are drawers of feet

and bins of hands." But there are no rooms
of feet on display, no rooms of hands pointing
or with grasps empty of staff, spear, thunderbolt.

And how could those compare to foreheads
precise with history, to these silent, knowing stares.
Heads without bodies. And somewhere, bodies

minus heads. Experts on such things arguing
for centuries over which goes where, about
the angle of face and neck, grain of stone,

color of marble, site of unearthing. Here, then,
the immortals, heroes, philosophers, ideas
we live by, even if they cannot be named.

PAOLA

Paola came to Athens from the Peloponnese
as a young man, a nondescript village, an ambitious boy.
"I have worked everything," he says,
pride riding his baritone like dolphins the ancient sea.
He is head waiter at Plaka Taverna on Kidathineon Street,
his words a sea eagle riding updrafts.
He doesn't care his people once defeated the Athenians.
Life is, after all, too good to gloat on such things.
Paola has a brother in Detroit, spent a year
washing dishes at his diner
and returned with enough money to marry.
We toast his success and eat our dinner,
this cheer conquering dusk, the tip
as generous as his bow.

#4729 SILVER DIADEM WITH DENTILATED BORDER

National Archeological Museum, Athens

This small crown, tarnished by age so that no gleam
shines through the glass display, rests with a dozen
other artifacts, shards of pottery, clay figurines,

mostly broken, and simple twists and coils of thin gold,
earrings, brooches, pins, all time-stained, redeemed
from Cyclades earth and reduced to catalogue number.

This crown exists without history, without metaphor.
It is itself, nothing more. But some father had wealth
and love enough to order this crown, to place it on

a daughter's head and smile at her new beauty,
which she, princess now, wore strolling the island's
agora above the rocky shore and stopping

to stare into the Aegean mist, where her dream
of love continued, him sailing through storm swells,
blown from island to island toward her,

without knowing this destiny she desired.
Each day she added more to the story, stared longer
in ankle-deep sea. Each day she prayed, first Artemis

then Aphrodite. Each day he drew closer in her heart.
But Herodotus is silent. She is without Homer.
No Sophocles. No god-shaped swan enfolded her

in feathers. No lyric entrusted to memory and chanted
at annual festival with song and sacrifice. No likeness
in marble with bare shoulders or breasts curving to shape

imaginations. No treasure unearthed with her bones.
Not even bones. Just a diadem on a glass shelf, dentilated,
grown darker each year. But once there was a dream

larger than an island and standing on its shore
a girl with dawnlight sprinkled in her crown.

AFTER THE REVELATION

Terpsichore and Clio from their
mountain perch look down upon Thebes,

see Jocasta trudging heavy-footed
in the palace courtyard while wetting

the dust with tears. The Dancer says,
"Ah, Jocasta, once you were light as air,

tripling from nursery to boudoir
and back. Your joy devoted to denials,

your husband-king both dead and alive.
It could not be, yet is. And now

the taste of such a life, such a lie stains
the very ground that sustained you.

You will dance on air again even if
the rhythm flows from a noose

and the measure of your life will be
skirt hems swaying without zephyr,

without the music of mourners."
And Clio vows to herself, "You,

the queen-prize, the mother-bride,
your story is patrimony's legacy."

(Thebes, 10/8/2008)

THE BUTCHER

On a table a leg of lamb. The butcher,
with left hand, lifts the bone end, turns
it slowly, trimming fat from this spot,
from that, and turns the leg again.

Time slows in the universe of this room.
When a customer enters the door open
to the street, he gentles leg and knife
to tabletop, wipes his greasy hands on

the half-clean smock, and wraps, distracted,
two lamb chops in paper for this young wife
so desperate to please a husband. He
returns to the low table, turning and

trimming as if his wrists connect to his soul,
as if marriage was a lesser pleasure.

Lavadia, Greece 10/8/2008

THE FLESH IN MARBLE

The Acropolis of Athens: "It took thirty years to build the most
perfect monuments in the history of the world."
—Sophia Kokkinou
The Most Famous Temples & Sanctuaries of Ancient Greece

i.

Mallet and chisel in strong hands carved this marble.
A freeman, artisan, enjoying bread and yogurt at day's end.
It was not the gods in the hand.
It was the full belly that frees the dreams reaching up, up,
          stones rising like smoke, like wind made solid, a miracle
          greater than Zeus become swan.
It was not lust after gods that raised columns, that anchored
          them in air with architrave as Archimedes said it would.
Clouds, shapeless, drifted away.
Maybe the temple did please Athena.
But it pleased the eyes of men more.
The dream of perfection.
It was the olive harvest plentiful at last.
When temple columns swell and lean with entasis to fool
          the eye, the gods gained nothing.
It was not magic but mathematics.
Even if the pediments were adorned with immortals, men
          made them.
Without Helen and Paris, what was Aphrodite.
Flesh and blood pumped the heavens into being.
Up and down the Acropolis, stones as broken as the gods.

ii.

It doesn't matter the number of years it takes to remake this
            once perfected place.
Imagine the joy in stone raised anew after centuries of disuse.
Behind the Parthenon, rows of cut stones and column drums,
            piled by size, marked by color, catalogued for guessed-at
            placement.
Then acres of marble dumped for later discovery.
Imagine the love in the hands of the student archeologist who
            matched two pieces of an Ionic capital in that rubble of marble.
When those carved swirls met at the fracture
            (ram horns from the mythological past)
            (back splash of waves against the rocky coast of a
            seafaring people),
what delight flamed her hands, her heart.
Imagine the tale told to coworkers at dinner
            (irrelevant food, just calories and carbohydrates,
            suddenly full of flavor)
            (the evening as bright as her moist eyes).
And we love her
            (without knowing her)
            because of this.
Because we love our stories and the tellers of stories.
Because of this the people aspired to the sky with marble offerings.
But this is less than calculus, less than olive groves planted on
            hillsides, less than semolina reaped and baked.
Even if we rebuild all the temples and all the theaters, what returns
            will not be divine ideals but human ideas.
Zeus was helpless when the earthquake toppled one of the twelve
            columns raised at his temple in the valley of Athens.
It was left there on the grass to remind us that the massive
            structures of man fall as easily as false dreams.
But we build them.
We build them.
It will be years until this joined stone shines atop a column to
            support that dream, that world no longer lived.
The sweat of what we once were will be more real.
The beauty extracted from living more real.

Poseidon and Athena will not wrestle again for our favor.
We have the trident.
The olive tree.
We no longer want a god breathing among us.
The eyes turning inward.
And look:
Here in the shade of old marble newly raised, a couple of teens
    on the stylobate steps kiss under the stony gaze of Karyatis.
What do years matter to young hearts of passion.

iii.

Homer and Herodotus, what more....
So many temples built and crashed, rebuilt and crashed again.
How lovingly the citizens of Athens buried their statues from
       the Persian threat.
After victory, with what pride did they dig them up, dust them,
       and set them in the sun where they belonged.
No wonder Greeks despise Lord Elgin stealing their art when it
       is more than artifice, more than sterling.
On the Acropolis today, the surface stone worn slick and slippery.
Generations of traffic from people who begged favor from god
       or king.
People who sought to mine wisdom from centuries.
People who wanted to touch human perfection in stone and
       know this struggle to be is worth it.
Because these marbles, these ideas are not Greek history, but our
       history.
Because Socrates under the shade of cedars and mulberries on
       the low side of this Acropolis did not preach.
He questioned.
Because Plato at the agora did not preach.
He told stories.

HOW THE CONQUERORS SETTLED

It is well known the Romans coveted
the bodies of Greek statues, the way
a discus thrower's back bulges and sways

against the immovable horizon, the soft
curve of Aphrodite's breasts, her dress
rippling to stone toes about to lift in dance,

but mostly they envied the grace of shoulders,
of buttocks soothing the ragged hills and
the rigid columns as the unforgiving summer

sun's shadow was leached of its harshness
by holy arm and calf muscles cast on
the parched ground, so that, as victors

settling into the next Hellenic city,
they removed the Greek heads and set atop
those worthy necks the stony brows of

Caesars and Hadrians, masters of all,
as long as they conquered a body
to mount their ambitions on.

PEACE

from the Greek of Bakcylides (5th century B. C.)

Great peace brings man wealth.
In honey-tongued throats, songs flower
as thigh-sliced oxen and long-haired sheep burn,
with golden flame, on crafted altars,
for the sake of the gods.
And young men who care more for flutes
and games gather round.

Black spiders build temples
in the idle handles of hidebound shields,
and spear and sword edges thicken with rust.
The bronze noise of trumpets sounding war
no longer strips the mind's sweet sleep,
and hearths stay warm.

And see, the hymns of children
fill the streets with a lovely blaze.

THE ANONYMOUS CLOSET

The dark is just the dark
where moons lack phase,
shadow upon faceless shadow.

The still air of being minus
the being itself where smile
is indulgence, lips of nothing.

Without Helen, no Hektor.
No death, no story. Only
Iphigenia growing old, bitter
in her anonymous closet.

An empty mountain throne.
Heroes everywhere silenced.
Slugs slugging along cold stone.

Let Briseis shout to all the warriors,
I am no man's prize as she withers
among dented armor. See:

Vultures rising on thermals.

BENEATH THE BLUE REALM

The daughter of the tavern owner on Mykonos only half smiles as she takes our order. She knows at this late hour Americans only want desert. Small fare. Tea and honey-cakes. She knows the tourist trade, lives it, inhales it, the lulls and rushes of dollars and euros, a stew of tongues swirling in and out her fair head, born and raised among these whitewashed homes and shops of stucco without edge, the sills rounded, the corners curved, and the wood trim blue as the Aegean sky at sunrise, a color so liquid and solid it could stop escape, as if anyone would leave this island except for another, except to flee an angry father whose daughter was soiled by a love and passion that was neither. Not even the old gods to help him, busy as they are up in that blue realm, keeping the eternity machine well-oiled. But this woman, tall, attractive, wedding-ring-less, widow-ring-less, indifferent to celestial mechanics, goes about the business of serving, smiling, gathering tips beneath the grapevine arbor that is a breathing roof above us, its great years laced in crisscrossed branches grown over all the trysts, the false pledges, the quick disappearances of handsome men. Soon we will board ship for Rhodes under a night sky that refuses to blacken, and we don't know it yet, but sea swells will rise until all thoughts of lovemaking drown and we'll huddle alone in perpendicular berths, yawing and pitching that counteracts romance, while she, on that rocky island, sleeps in a steady bed, solitary or not, dreaming or not dreaming.

SMYRNA

Once on the rocky shore
        of Smyrna a man
                squatted in the fuzz of waking

Time waiting on wet rocks
        like a monster or a goddess
                There was a wind

that arrested the fog
        and hauled it off
                like shorepolice a drunken sailor

A dark line vertical in the harbor
        Rib bone of ship
                sunken before alphabets

Perhaps a miscalculation
        that hypnotic singing
                the ropes torn and Odysseus free

to grab the tiller
        to steer into the song
                the song kissing the hull

hard as rocks hard as truth and the crew
        the crew like a chorus
                fading to silence

The man filled his palms with beach sand
        Again and again it drained
                through holes in flesh in hours

no stone could plug
        no story could satisfy
                as an echo burbling in foamy sea

Oh, Homer, we die
        for glory Do us
                honor Remember honor

Where men dig at the shores
    there the secrets lie
        We make them truths

BELLY DANCER

When she finishes with a flourish and holds
that pose some seconds before she sits
at the empty table beside the dance floor,
crude sticks and boards to square those curves,
to contain that energy—
                              the physics of sweat
weaving through time and that glistening
black hair pulled tight from the geometry of
her forehead—
                              and because this dance is art,
a generation seems to pass into dust before
those serious lips loosen to smile, to
the finality of fingers curling inward,
clutching itself, as if afraid all those
undulations of flesh could escape.

Izmir

BRISEIS IN MIDTOWN

In the patience assumed at bus stops,
you stand without talking
to others, knowledge drawn in,
as natural as breathing.

Lives ago you stood at some fountain
where old women's gossip
was the skill young girls learned; that
and the weight of water.

This same city wind
was there, blowing from Mt. Ida
to touch the market square. And if one glanced
away from the fountain waters

to face the sea breeze
as if to question
the horizon, to live
a minute or two in dutiless dream,

perhaps it was you,
as today these winds fall
between tall buildings and glaze your eyes
that long beyond us here.

STEALING TROY

i.

The bloody sun settling into the Aegean
beyond the ruins of Troy kisses stone
broken and shattered for love, for pride,

while in the east a full pale moon begins
to gloat over it all, the way Artemis coldly
heard wailing and sobbing till wells

ran dry, till walls crumbled and bloodlines
ended, devoured by dusty earth, and she,
appeased at Aulis, turned her back upon

humanity and walked into the hills where
deer and boar curled about her feet to sleep
the sound, dreamless sleep of animals.

But look: In Troy there are stones scorched
by fire, scattered across the hill by earthquake
and scavengers, stone that held king and queen

in their conceit, spectators atop walls
as their sons dropped one by one.
At night joyless stars fell into the sea

without hiss, without grief. Poseidon
embarrassed momentarily, a blink in eternity.
Then he, too, gone. By day a thousand men

obeying race, one after the other, fallen
to dust. Pillars, arches, stone goddesses
crashing down as up rose the sobs and wails

of Cassandra's sisters, each a prize carried
to a foreign land, each vanishing into the blotter
of history. But here, standing in these ruins

today, raise a stone shard, set it to ear,
and the swords clashing echo, the crying
echoes until your ears want to bleed.

Blame a father's honor, a brother's honor.
Blame the lust and love the gods
inspire and envy so that, today, neither

the blood of passion nor the blood of
courage stain this soil, these broken stones
the rains of ages blotch without mercy.

ii.

Wind in the cypress, in the wild olive laughing
at honor, at flesh and bone, at their delusion of permanence.

Grass and wildflower germinating in the widening
cracks and fissures of Troy, its stones split, charred, scattered.

Marble columns buried and broken
like stone worms, breathless, unable to undulate.

Marble walks smothered in upheaved earth and vegetation,
only jaw bone of cat, tibia of mouse, whitened on the ground.

Blame the lichen its gradual, millennial meal on stone,
the grains of sand blowing from sea shore to explode on stone.

Troy fallen to blood, to fire, to disguised avarice,
for the greater good of Agamemnon, and all that.

Nine times Troy rose and fell to anger, to pestilence,
to erosion, to the cloudy memory of men.

Look: Aphrodite dancing her jealous dance on Mt. Ida
with her one promise for the one boy tending his father's sheep.

Look: Helen dancing the fire dance in the temple about to fall
and she succumbs, again, as plaything of men and gods.

Look: Sofia Schliemann, adorned and aglitter in gold,
posing and dancing for a husband's delight and desire.

Once, the walls were golden in the sunset.
Once, the sea shimmered against the Plains but withdrew,

the horror of tides without amanuensis.
Tides of blood and wailing rose and fell in the breath swell

of women dancing their desperation, dancing into destiny.
City and field deserted, plundered.

Walk in the ruins of Troy today and feel the years,
themselves, crumbling through the heart.

iii.

By the time the German who loved Homer arrived,
Troy was not even Troy in 1871, a dusty hill, hints of marble.
The Ottomans had stolen its name, called it Hisserlik
and forbid all from walking its grassy slopes.
But the German dug deep and took treasure to Athens
then Berlin and the local Turks hauled down large stones
for the bridge over River Simois. Passion and practicality
serving each other. And for a while, Homer became
real, read anew, new dreams inspired. The German
who loved Homer divorced the Russian mother
of his children to marry an unseen girl from Athens.
And Priam's Treasure glowed behind glass to applause
until another war.
                    When the smoke cleared over Berlin,
the Soviets found that gold, removed it from history.
For fifty years rumors and speculation filled lecture halls
and the trenches at digs of those trying to make
the ancient world live again in stone, in glory.
But Troy dismantled under torch light is not glory.

The stones are scattered among buildings in the towns
within sight of the hill, fragments of carved marble stuccoed
in their walls, in sills and lintels.
                                    At the road side stop
outside Troie, I photograph a child, her mother,
her grandmother, age ninety-five, the van driver
tells me; they smile though the child seems puzzled—
how does mere existence elicit a camera's praise?
But it is the marble in the doorstoop I capture.
Here, people live with shards of Troy stone gracing
homes even if they don't know it, even if their Ionian blood
is so thin Arachne couldn't weave it into a small web, because
that ancient courage, that passion that builds and destroys
abides in the ground they walk, the air they breathe, as today,
descending through diggings into earthen holes where dry
stone walls support only myth and belief, I breathed
beyond the musty ruin, beyond the wind-blown horizon,
lungs and heart expanding, contracting, expanding.

iv.

Today, a wooden horse at the entrance to Troy,
            a caricature of the lust and deceit of men,
so tourists can climb a wooden ladder and stand
            inside the belly of story and pretend to know
Odysseus, pretend to feel his fierce cunning,
            that devotion to the Greeks, that poetry in his blood.

Causation and adventure confused in the soul
            and excused by the heart.

If only it were that simple. How can we erase
            the bronze weight of sword and helmet
from our ascent into the belly of history,
            of storied history?
The only burden today, perhaps, a paperback Homer
            in the pocket and an aching in the breast.

How many have come here from such longing?

Xerxes sacrificed a thousand bulls to Troy-Athena
before crossing the Hellespont.
                              Alexander, in honor,
ran naked, thrice, around the tomb of Achilles.

                                        When
Julias Caesar came to Novum Ilium, he was warned,
        "Do not offend the ghost of Hector."
But Caesar only saw ruins and darkness and left
for the promise of Egypt.
                        Emperor Julian praised Ajax,
from whom he claimed descent, by digging up his bones
        to bury again with flourish and trumpet,
flags and parade, speeches that no one wrote down
        so that they are less than rumor,
less than the dust carried in Aegean breeze.

All in homage of Aeneas who fled Troy's fire and the wrath
        of gods to start it all over again somewhere else.

Students on hands and knees sweating
        with trowel and brush
to dig and clean around stones and shards of stones,
        while others haul blocks to place on low walls
reconstructed by professors,
        who argue among themselves as they sit in the shade
beneath canopies and occasionally toast each other with cognac
        as dark as blood spilled,
but not today.
                Today, shepherds tend flocks of sheep grazing
in the fields of blood fed grasses.

Today the tourists follow guides around
        fallen columns
to graze on history for thirty minutes
        before getting back on buses
to the next spectacle of ruins.

Walls of stone were raised in glory,
        and fell in seasons of defeat.
One after another, the story repeats,
        like course after course
of brick and stone in those walls,
        rising, falling, rising, falling.

        In the ruins of Troy, you can feel Time,
itself, multiplied, while rodents in the cracks
        of civilization feast upon each other.

II.

A KISS BEHIND THE CAMPIDOGLIO

What matter is a full moon gracing this horizon,
showering its cool light upon the cold marble?
Yes, it is beautiful. But ghostly. More a gasp,
less a sigh. Not something Botticelli would
clothe with color. More fit for film noir—
>   *a man meets on the street*
>   *a woman he once loved;*
>   *a simple hug and brush of lips on cheek;*
>   *they walk a little without speaking;*
>   *eyes moist; cigarette ash growing;*
>   *this same forum as background. . .*
You and I make it real with a kiss
in the still warm Roman night.
To the south we see the Colosseum
with upper arches glowing in subdued light,
as if they once held up the heavens
and were crushed. Tomorrow we will climb
its broad steps to the top, look down on Rome
like visiting dignitaries, frame a few pictures,
believe we hear the clash of swords
and lions roar. But tonight we stand on
concrete that will not last two thousand years.
When the bus that has a few hints of rust
arrives, we board it, return to the hotel
and dream the dream of immortality.

Note: Rome's Campidoglio has been the seat
of government since ancient times.

VILLA POMPHILI PARK

Rome

This is where the mothers go
Sunday afternoon, pushing strollers full of sleep.
        They hold a toddler's hand
as he carries a stone rescued from the dirt path,
        or watch their kindergartner
running ahead, back, and off again until a bee
        startles the little girl
and she cries, *mama mama*, and mother squats,
        opens her arms, gathers
all those tears to her until the child smiles
        and runs off toward tomorrow.

There are no children in downtown Rome.
        The mothers here are women,
elegant, fashionable, aware of men's eyes.
        It is in the park that maternity
matters, even as teenage boys pass a soccer ball near
        the university students reciting
love poetry. And there, some philosopher,
        or retired mechanic,
strolls with hands behind his back, his eyes
        bruised with tomorrow.

An elderly husband pushes the wheelchair
        that hugs his wife.
The way he wipes the sweat from her brow
        says love. He turns back
to the shade as if only a few minutes of sun
        is the wife's allotment.
You wonder if he secretly wants to leave her
        in the park, shaded or not,
and for a moment be the man he once was.
        The way she pats
the back of his wet hand lets him know
        there will be a tomorrow.

Umbrella Pines line the paths. Bought by
        old wealth, planted
and groomed by servants according to a plan.
        They are tall, shady,
and do look like umbrellas, held aloft in Juno's hands,
        so that, walking beneath them,
you feel waited upon, important, maybe in the manner
        of a duke and duchess from yesterday.

Once you could walk here at sunset,
        a country respite,
look from this grassy rise, see St. Peter's dome
        and believe. See marbled
Rome glow in last light as if time has no end.
        Today the sky's haze
bounds you just to this plot of greenery
        servants once tended,
with sons and daughters born to do the same.
        But that was yesterday.

Today civil servants mow and trim. Today
        the paved roads,
the apartments, stores and shops, gas stations
        and co-ops of the city
crowd the villa's walls. The Pomphili family
        no longer live here.
They gifted the villa and its vast grounds
        to the city and moved
with their servants and their families to
        il dutchy denominato Ieri.

HISTORY AS HOBBY

We climb worn marble stairs
into a night of glaring electric lamps.
Castor and Pollux greet us
in marble, naked, thrice as tall as a man;
to the side of each
a pony as pale as the moon.
Then a bronze Marcus Aurelius,
right arm stretched in salute,
silent equestrian dominating the square.
Michelangelo moved him here
as honor, even though his gold
was robbed, melted down
to serve others' pleasures.
Empires rise and fall;
nations fade or reform.
Aurelius knew this and watches,
says nothing, this last great stoic.
We walk through
Piazza del Campidoglio, leave this century
to stand at a stone wall
overlooking the Roman Forum,
ruins from the first century
backlit like some stage set sunken
in an urban valley excavated
beneath brick, stone, stucco.
Only a few columns stand
between temple arches raised
so moderns can imagine the festivals
of Vespasian and Saturn,
the singing, girls twirling,
braziers glowing long into the night.
Cows once grazed there;
peasants squatted in huts;
it was their right,
until Caesar forced them out.
The public good, he said,
demanded columns, façades,
speeches and celebrations.
Now shattered stone, now dust

is preserved by government decree,
history as hobby, reclaimed
as time, as money allow.
      No Legions march victorious
beneath the Arch of Septimius Severus,
returning victorious from campaigns
in Palatine.
      No crowds ecstatic in cheer,
just tourists bunched like vegetables
atop a cart in the market square.
      The applause is elsewhere,
for a few tenors and sopranos,
for leather steering wheels
tightly held at 200 kph,
before they sit to pasta, bread, and
a bottle of deep, dark Castello Banfi.

IN THE SISTINE CHAPEL

i. Inventing secret signs

Look up at all those penises
resting aside the ample thighs
of angels (Oh, bless their holy members!),
and of important men, *consiglieri* to God or princes.
These are not the Italians, dark and handsome,
of the movies. These are *Romani*,
competing with Medici and the Milanese.
But all that flaccid maleness—
even our progenitor,
Adam,
doesn't have it up.
According to the story, he didn't have to
yet. That came later.
How much later no one knows.
It's not like counting the generations
back to Moses, which also occurred much later.
And not like the (very) early christians, before
the Capitalization of words,
as they clandestinely carried themselves and
Peter's bones,
from place to hiding place, living,
themselves, underground, both literally and
figuratively, inventing
such things as:
                   secret signs
                   small, wooden crosses
                   the catacombs,
(thank God,
for volcanic rock beneath Rome
that readily succumbed
to stick, pilfered metal rod, or even
thumbnail); and not the same as later
Christians (Capital letter by now)
who argued over the genuflect—
its form, its length:
only one
knee on the ground; head lowered; and not

too long a duration, else
a charge of excessive piousness; anyway
this obeisance neater, cleaner
than prostration, so that
it allowed the development of
                button front shirts
                pleated slacks,
                the miniskirt,
though banned from this chapel
for three generations, as were women regardless of dress
before then. Imagine those first women allowed,
how they struggled not to glance
heavenward with all those penises awaiting,
and how, of course, they did, and what stories they told, later.

ii. Standing beneath the creation of man

Michelangelo put donkey ears
on a bishop on the wall in the Sistine Chapel.
Considering the scope of the work,
a minor detail, unless it was you
so insulted, which,
thank God,
it wasn't.
But the bishop voiced a protest
to his Holiness.
And did not the Pope
tell the bishop, "Sit down, *signore*. It is
only metaphor."

And what of that devil, on the same wall,
the one whose skeletal face stares straight at
you,
pensively, with still fleshy hand on boney chin,
with a flash of irony in those empty eye sockets,
and an almost smile
to the way
the lower jaw hinges on maxilla?
Standing there didn't the skin become sweaty
and the head dizzy?
Didn't you try to turn away
but could not?
Didn't you try to laugh it off

until the guards
approached with official faces
and that was what it took for you to walk away
and stand in the center of the chapel,
beneath the creation of man,
which is where you belong anyway, and perhaps where
that bishop stood, still complaining, first to the artist,
then His Eminence, who was about to speak
when the artist said, "Hee Haw."
Which brings us back to metaphor and
those fingers, high above,
about to touch.

iii. "If God hath a beard"

Imagine the artist's barrel-chested
laugh as he drew and painted
on the ceiling God's Ass.
This is not metaphor, but the real
Holy Behind exposed
when His tunic rode up His Back
as He leaned over the cloud
to separate light from darkness.

Can you hear laughter echoing
the length of that tall, long chapel
and rolling down the halls?
Did not even the Pope,
Julius II, three
buildings away, hurry, abandoning decorum,
along the connected corridors to the echo's source?

Mighten the artist have replied
to His Eminence's inquiries, "If God
hath a beard, hath He not, then, an ass?"
Imagine the Pope nodding his head,
almost smiling as he told the artist:
"Continue, *mio amico*. Continue."
And Michelangelo did.

THE COLOSSEUM

Granite steps too broad for comfort,
but up we go to the circular walk,
eyes adjusting to the Roman sun.
Here, above interior ruins,
extends the shell of the top two levels,
the scale of it hurries breath;
the massive, ancient genius, the labor.
In the skeleton below us—
stone ribs appealing to the sky,
walls and pillars, arches and rubble.
Animals and gladiators breathed there,
in dark corridors beneath a wooden
floor rotted or pilfered centuries ago.

A marble-dusted cricket crawls
across my leather shoe, squeezes
into a chink between stones and
disappears. And I realize
that some cricket will always
fracture the air, that then is now.

IN THREE LANGUAGES

I'm riding in a cab from the outskirts
to the center of Rome. The driver has
no English. I have only a few phrases
from the guide book, *Quando
il treno va? Que Costa?* We idle
in bundled lines. The museum
closes in an hour. Exhaust, horns
and shouting surround us,
but the silence inside the cab
as thick as the traffic outside.
When the light changes,
everyone rushes to the next wait
a few dozen metres ahead.
I say to myself, I think, *Bitte,
mach schnell.* The driver hears this,
says, *Sprechen Sie Deutsch?* When
I answer, *Ya, ein bisschen Deutsch.
Sind Sie amerikaner?* he asks.
Again *Ya.* And, *Sind Sie italiener?*
It is his turn to say, *Ya.* Our eyes
meet in the rear view mirror
and we laugh. We drive like this,
the American tourist talking
German to the Italian cabdriver.
I tell Rosario I learned German
thirty years ago when I was
a soldier stationed in Germany.
He drove cab in Zurich for three
years thirty years ago.
We toast each other in three
languages. He asks what is at
the address I gave him in writing.
I tell him it is a museum for
an English poet who, being a true
gentleman, left England to die in Rome.
Rosario likes that, even if he doesn't
know it is not quite true, and says,
"Those English! Most people come
to Rome for *amore*, but not the English.

They are so cold." I ask why he used
the Italian for love and not the German.
He says, "*Liebe* is a good word, but
amore is Rome." The German on both
our tongues is rusty and we blurt
out phrases as they come to us.
I try to tell him of another
English poet who came
to Italy with his English bride,
also a poet, because they knew
Rome is the place for love.
He tells me *L'amore è Roma*
is the phrase. I thank him, tell him
the bride is buried in Firenze, that
I am going there tomorrow.
When I leave the cab, we wish
each other only good luck,
gutes Glück, buona fortuna.

OUTSIDE THE KEATS-SHELLEY HOUSE

Piazza di Spagna 26, Rome

I was saying softly the first Keats
poem I'd read: the maiden, the grace
of her kiss frozen in unwilting youth
is such a melody fixed in memory.
Taxis were arriving and people exited
to join the crowd gathering on
the Spanish Steps, each one striding
higher up to fit in, each man brandishing
a bottle of dark wine. But I just stood
in front of this building, thinking
of how time tricks us with promise,
then lies about death the way we can see
the light in shade but not the shade in light.
I imagined Keats returning from
the *Biblioteca* after hours reading and
scribbling in letters: *all die young.*
I watched him climb the stone stairs
to the door, pause, body bent in spastic
coughs until he leaned against that cold wall.
He stood shaking in the building's shadow,
his face angel-pale, with whom, by now,
he was intimate in the dark paradise
of his routine. He unlatched the door,
disappeared inside. As I walked over
the threshold, the revelers on the Steps
beamed into song, a hundred voices
celebrating the fortune of their evening.
When I tried to follow Keats up the stairs
to his room, he kept ascending.

SAINT MATTHEW IN THE STONE

Florence

What was it Michelangelo saw
in the heart of his Matthew
that he abandoned him in Carrara marble,
struggling to be free, to stand in air,
to be almost man yet more than man?
The months of chipping away white flecks of stone
came to nothing. Michelangelo walked away.
He left Matthew's leg bent at the knee
trying to step from his marble prison,
anguish frozen in his unfinished eyes.
The sculptor blind to such a plea.
Not even the half formed Gospel, hinting at God's breath,
held high in Matthew's left hand,
could urge him back to mallet and chisel.
So Matthew stands today crowded in a museum corridor,
an unfinished prelude to the masterpiece,
to David haloed in light, solitary, regal.
Michelangelo found something dark
deep in the heart of that stone,
then walked away.

RUINS

Milan

We walk the Galleria, admire
    this year's
    women's fashions —
black upon black,
    dark as a Sicilian maid's eyes.

We find a department store,
wander among
    leather furniture
    kitchen appliances
    dinnerware.

We buy a set of *gelato* spoons
    for our daughter
    to serve guests ice cream
with elegance.

At the camera shop
    more postcards.

We notice down a side alley
    a section roped off.

We walk there,
    see a large gap
    in the asphalt.

We lean against the ropes,
    look into the hole —
    ten feet below the street
cobbles neatly pave another street.

Broken columns
    on their sides.
Blocks of cut stone
    scattered in front of a low wall
    of the same stone
laid three and four courses high.

A pair of work gloves down there.
Two red hard hats.

A city beneath the city.

We wonder
        how old it is,
        how they found it.

Did a water main break,
        flush away the earth and rubble
        of millennia
before the street collapsed,
        revealing its secret —
        a forgotten life
alive only in text books, in lectures?

How the university professors
        and city engineers
        must have hurried here,
hands sweaty in anticipation.

Did that evening's headlines declare
        Ancient Ruins Beneath Shopping District?

But there is only this small piece
        of the old world
        unearthed,
room for only a few workers
        to descend
        into the past.

Imagine if beneath this whole part of the city
        the first Milan
        hibernates?
It will remain so.

How could all these shops and offices
        be dismantled,
        clerks and accountants sent home,
just to dig up
        carved stone,
        marble
in a country full of relics?

How much history
        can a culture endure
        before it forgets to live today
and regrets itself?

You cannot walk,
        especially the first time
        in a foreign city,
by watching your shoes,
        by questioning
        the very ground
beneath you —

you will only see
        shadows growing
and miss the sun declining
        beyond the cathedral's spires.

LEONARDO

Milan

From the brighter light
        at the end
        of this row of buildings,
a piazza opens to the sky.

We round the corner, smile
        at its ample space,
breathe the scent
        of linden trees, some pink
        and red chrysanthemums
and grass
        trim as small lawns
        between sidewalks.
People sitting
        on benches or grass.

But the statue
        in the center
        dominates.
We stand before it and do not need
        to trouble
        over lengthy inscriptions —
the cardinal letters proclaim

Leonardo

        tall, bearded,
        scholar's robe flaring
        as if to encircle the world.

Is that reverence
        in the faces of these people?
Admiration
        for this first modern man?

Some Americans off
        to the side,
        talking loudly
as they munch
        from a paper bag.

If I say

        Benjamin,

who would know Franklin is my model?

If I say

        Jack,

                who could guess
                JFK is in my thoughts?

Perhaps mentioning

        Olivier

                in a crowded room
                will turn the conversation to Oscars.

But just whisper

        Leonardo

                and a woman's half smile
                fills the Louvre

        Leonardo

                and you scribe a circle around
                the sketch of a naked man
                in perfect balance

Leonardo

> and you hold a notebook
> against a mirror,
> write in secret code

Leonardo

> and you stand on the cliffs
> above the bay at Genoa
> sketching seagulls in flight.

JULIET ON THE BALCONY

Verona

For years the people here offered their balconies as Juliet's.
And town fathers searched every street to find
the one balcony that fit the story.
And they did. Pronouncements were made.
A plaque erected. A statue commissioned. It is here
in this little courtyard through an arched alley of a back street
now crowded with shops, trattorias, tourists.
Everyone looking for love.
And we also came in a bus full of seekers.

Declarations in many languages are scratched
on the old stone walls of this courtyard.
I saw *amore* in one and you *liebe* in another.
There are scraps of paper glued to the stones
with phone numbers and email addresses.
So many starved for love.

A bronze Juliet stands demurely at the end of the courtyard.
Couples line up for a picture with her.
Each man cups a hand on the statue's right breast.
Her small bronze mound
glows after years of such a touch.

For two euros Natalie gets to climb two flights of stairs
then stand on Juliet's balcony.
She waves to the crowd below in the courtyard
but her smile is for me.
I snap the photograph and ask myself if I would scale
that wall to steal a kiss from Juliet.

All this, of course, is not real, not authentic.
Romeo never climbed this wall, never said
But soft, what light through yonder window breaks...
It is my Juliet. It is my love.
But I said it, almost shouted it
when you appeared up there, waved to the crowd
and smiled at me.

10-17-03

THE BRIDGE OF SIGHS

How many men walked this bridge,
shackles clanking on stone, stooping
at the low stone door, one minute
in the paneled courtroom full of Doges
deciding fates and the next condemned,
straight to jail, to darkness, to perdition?

I have walked the Bridge of Sighs glad
I was a tourist, one among many trying
to imagine last glances at fathers or wives,
a futile plea for air fresh and flowing
over water where these stones arched,
where those men ached with each step.

An Englishman called it the Bridge of Sighs
when he rode these mephitic canals
under the unrelenting sun, dark eyes
staring down from behind stone, iron,
and desperation. For him, a mere quip,
a moment that lasted, became a truth.

Did he, too, walk the Bridge of Sighs,
tipping the gaoler for entrance and exit,
a quick trip through hell's elevated
passageway, one more experience in his
delicate world of fancy, his nobility
an insult to inmates, to destiny?

I have walked the Bridge of Sighs, fingers
tracing initials carved in walls, eyes widening
at such small, rusty cells, at stains blended
into floor paint, my own loud exhale
an echo of whimper, an instant only in
the quickening of all the lives wasted here.

Venice, 10-19-2003

ONE DAY IN THE APENNINES

Caprese, Italy

i.
What isn't stone or plowed earth is green
in these mountains, field tobacco shivering
in late morning light, bright fig trees
on hillsides, netting stretched beneath them
to catch the sweet fruit and save the backs and legs
of old men. A few pigs and sheep forage on slopes
so precarious death smiles. Some valley floors
are flat and farmers there feel blessed,
live longer; some sell a few acres and new
houses are laced into the landscape—
for the first time in generations, city people
move to the country and begin to fall in love,
as long as the train to Rome runs twice a week.

ii.
In these mountains all exalt the village of Caprese,
it is the mother of Umbrian pride—there, years ago,
a farmer's wife sliced olives and tomato,
added them to garden greens, sprinkled it with oil
and Romano to invent salad for her men;
menus across Italy honor that village
with its name scripted on their tinted pages.
But before that, in 1473, a minor government
official was quietly transferred to that village;
it was not an auspicious post;
a son was born to him
there, who became
Michelangelo.

III.

FRANCIS d'ASSISI 2008

*Many people also desire material wealth and dream of money, but
St. Francis teaches every one of us, whatever our social condition
may be, to fight against "the lust of the eyes", which is full of deceit
and vanity. The wealth of Christian life does not consist in money
and all its cares and demands. To some extent it is necessary for our
very existence, but we must not lose our hearts to it. In the presence
of his father and of the Bishop, Francis gave up everything, even the
clothes he was wearing — such was his love for poverty.*

—Pope John XXIII

I.

When a young man saw the beggar's rags,
did he offer his coat with the words,
"Forgive the gold thread its glitter"?

When the young man's father saw this,
did he think as he had the boy arrested,
"He shall not inherit my fortune"?

Because he could not sleep in jail,
the young man prayed away the hours, the days,
and in those rhythms, found happiness, peace.

When he left that cell,
did he search for the well-dressed beggar,
did he thank him?

II.

i.

Because his thoughts could be unclean,
the young man built a stone chapel

in the wilderness of the Umbrian Plain
to pray and purge himself,

to contain that other wildness, that doubt,
within those short walls

of gathered stone and wood, earthen floor
to rest his head. Three meters by four,

enough to watch the lives of animals,
enough to hear God in birdsong,

enough to wander in the wild grasses,
tramping the hillsides

among trees thick and dark,
each step a line of prayer toward light,

each pause a verse,
even unto his own prayers composed

under rain, or with the approval of Brother Sun
upon his cropped head,

even unto the witness of a doe birthing a fawn
in a florid clearing in the dark forest—

What man would then forgive
the wolves their hunger,

what shepherd could their torn sheep?
Francis forgave.

There are wolves no longer
in Umbria,

that hunger extinct,
the sheep safe in the fold.

ii.

The people see birds eat
from the hand of a solitary monk

who preached to them. And the birds listened,
perched in the trees, on his hand,

atop his head. Afterward
birds sang and the monk transcribed the songs.

The people tell others of that
fearlessness,

who tell others
until young men

who want to believe
arrive.

iii.

Came Bernard of Quintaville.
Came Sabatinus and Moricus.
Came Ferdinand from Lisbon
       who went forth to convert the Muslims,
        but got sick. Yet still he believed, and worked,
        sacrificed, and became Saint Anthony.
Came John of Capella, who afterwards went away.
Came Philip and four others.
Came Clare, young heiress of Assisi,
       and Francis cut her hair, received her
       into poverty, penance, seclusion,

this in the year of the Children's Crusade.

Came her sister Agnes with another.
More maidens arrived, holiness in the eyes.
Francis cut their hair, made them
The Order of the Poor Clares,
        who still today pray for us.
Came Juniper, a jester,
        who carried fame
        inside a bag of poverty.
Came the Three Companions:
        Angelus, a cavalier,
        Rufinus, who was cousin of Clare,
        Leo, confessor to Francis,
                who shared the forty days
                feasting on prayer
                in the last year of Francis,
        Leo, the confessor,
                who witnessed the stigmata.

And each wrote
        the life of Francis that they knew.

                        iv.

And Pope Innocent III dreamed a poor man
would come to him from Assisi

and Francis came to him with eleven followers
and Innocent gave sanction to their Rule:

Poverty, Chastity, Obedience.

They wandered forth
two by two from place to place

like children singing
their joy.

v.

Came Peter of Cattaneo,
  who would gather the lepers
  and Francis prayed with them
  and ate off their plates.
Came Masseo,
  who accompanied Francis,
  two by two, preaching, praying.
Came Pacificus, who in the world
  had been a poet.

vi.

And Francis, himself, went
to convert the Muslims,

and he, too,
became ill—food too rich,

prayers too public, too prolific,
the line between deep, irrevocable.

vii.

But Francis kept wandering, preaching
in Italy, in the vernacular, never alone.

Clergy and townspeople paraded
behind him as he walked into their village.

He stood in the marketplace, a magnet,
on church steps, a magnet

or from the walls of castle courtyards,
a magnet.

Enraptured, church bells sounded.
Enraptured, people sang.

They brought their sick for him to bless, to heal.
They kissed the ground on which he trod.

They cut pieces of his tunic
until he left the village poorer

and richer.

viii

In twenty years five thousand Brothers, more on
       their way.
So many that more Rules were needed:

> *Let those who have promised obedience take one tunic
> with a hood, let those who wish it have another without
> a hood. And those who must may wear shoes.*

And

> *Whatever house they enter, they are first to say,
> "Peace to this house."*

And

> *In their preaching the words of the brothers should be
> studied and chaste, useful and edifying to the people,
> telling them about vices and virtues, punishment and
> glory; and they ought to be brief, because the Lord kept
> his words brief when he was on earth.*

until Twelve Rules for living were approved
in Rome.

ix.

And Honorius III gave Francis *il perdono d'Assisi*
which is an indulgence

the Brothers could sell,
but not for money, and only one day a year,

but there is no record
of this indulgence, only

the *argumentum ex silentio*
and rumors give proof,

so precious are
such things,

as if the future of the Church
depended on them.

x.

Then Francis to Damietta with the Crusaders
who were victorious. Then he walked

across the battlefield line to those infidels
to convert the Sultan,

who agreed to better conditions for prisoners
but nothing else

and Francis returned knowing only God
could do better, thus satisfied with this promise,

until he learned that in Rome they were saying
Francesco è guasto,

that he believed no longer
Poverty, Chastity, Obedience.

xi.

In Venice, Francis saw the Brothers
neither working nor fasting
and grew alarmed

and gave the Order to Peter of Cattaneo,
so he could fill the days with prayer alone
where he once found happiness

but Peter died soon after,
and still they came.
Came many new Brothers

and Francis could not teach
them all. So he walked into a field,
knelt, prayed as they watched,

prayed for hours, while they, expectant.
Francis would call this
Silent Teaching.

xii.

And Francis this time gave the Order
to Brother Elias, ever faithful.
Then Francis to the mountain of *La Verna*,
gift of Count Orlando, who was a believer.

This mountain such
una roccia robusta, in the style of Dante,
a perfect retreat and Francis prayed there
for forty days, fasting all the while.

So subservient the meditation
that the wounds of Christ blossomed on his body.
This the Pope would call *The Stigmata*.
And Leo was witness.

Tomorrow and tomorrow, Francis more frail,
his body less than whispered prayer, his breath.
Came Lady Jacoba, who nursed with prayer and waited
to the end, though women were forbidden,

and Francis, grateful,

called her Brother Jacoba.

Then Francis buried on the hill
of sinners and thieves.

III.

Because they are Italian and Catholic
and wanted to show reverence,
frescos were painted on the little chapel
after its builder died. Carved doors
with heavy hinges bit into mortar.
Then frescos on the inside, vaulted even onto heaven,
and a statue, pews, candles and crucifix.
In the joy of labor, gold was purchased.
Soon a village of believers settled down
to till the rich, alluvial soil and pray,
in the name of Francis.

Because the people feared the wind
that swayed the hem of Francis's robe,
and the rain that danced on his bare feet
would ruin the colors in the frescos,
they built their church around his chapel,
and used the chapel as tabernacle and altar,
and stood or kneeled inside their brick and granite
that sheltered the chapel,
like the heart inside the chest of Christ.

Soon enough there grew a city,
then high stone walls burgeoned
over simple houses and fields.
The people sacrificed for marble and glass
for their church, a grandeur to match their faith.

More pilgrims in the dawn's light, carrying their belief
across mountains, up rivers; they ate and drank
until their money was spent;
they worked for bakers, brick makers,
married the daughters.

Because some begged on the cobbled streets
the Brothers took them in, taught them
to sing, to pray in Latin, to clean the altars,
trim the candles and carry the coins.

The Brothers and the people tore down the folksy church
that cradled the simple chapel,
quarried whole hillsides for marble,
in the name of Francis,
mined clay banks from rivers to bake into bricks, stacked them
taller and wider for the bronze and marble,
in the name of Francis,
bought with gold gifted by noble families
who only wanted side altars in their names
and prayers in perpetuity for their salvation,
in the name of Francis.

Came Giotto, at great expense, to make
the life of Francis live on these walls,
though his colors, today, are faded.

Thus a cathedral in the once wilderness
sitting tall on the flat plain with a new bishop
anointed, though not in the tradition of Francis:
Poverty, chastity, obedience
a trinity not always heeded by these times,
the memory of Francis fading.

IV.

Because he wanted to be humble
even after death, Francis willed his burial
on the *Colle d'Inferno* with the thieves and murderers.

All this done, though to great consternation
of the faithful, who desired marble and gold
to signify the wealth of their faith.

There was no peace
for the corpse
of the man who preached peace.

Exhumed, re-interred in altar stone,
they built a chapel around the body,
a church around the chapel, there on the hill,

then a basilica to compare with any in Italy,
with schools, monastery,
cloistered order of nuns still praying for us,

and a town of shopkeepers, butchers, maids, carpenters,
and all atop this hill became *locus sanctorum.*
Came Brother Elias, the Faithful Companion,

who stole the body
and buried it in the church below the hill
for protection against mourners so fervent

they would steal a bone
and Elias, too, passed, his secret
untold.

Six centuries Francis lay there
unknown, undisturbed,
at peace.

ii.

Because the morning sun rose in the high basilica window
and blasted the altar with cruel light
the church fathers sent

to Scotland and Holland for artisans
who were rumored to color glass
and join pieces into a prayer of light.

The artisans arrived to the songs of the first
raven haired maidens they'd ever seen or kissed
and to the first dark wines soothing their palate.

They cut glass, stained it,
and fixed it into a rose in that window.
The light of the world was softened.

This the first church in all the country
with such a window, this, itself,
a thing to admire.

> *(A thing blessed by God for all years, the people said
> after the pre-millenial earthquake cracked the floor and
> walls and vaulted ceiling, showered stone and debris
> onto worshippers, who hurried to God and all the
> saints or to satan and his demons, but could not break
> the soul of that prized window. A miracle they sang.
> And prayed. The next day's sun spilled on the mute
> blood of the faithful and the living beseeched for mercy
> and eternal life in the name of Francis.)*

iii.

And pilgrims came. Simple folk
who heard about the simple monk and approved,
who prayed, found work and a wife,

or who bought a cross or two to bring back
to their mountain village where all would pray
for a good harvest and gentle weather,

in the name of Francis

And the cathedral looked up to the basilica
on the hill and approved.
And the basilica's bells rang and echoed

the voices up and down the valley,
people and animals at night,
singing in praise.

Each year people came to pray and to touch the stone
on the altar where Francis was not buried,
though they did not know.

And in the great age of global leisure,
tourists came, more and more each year,
and with them hotels, restaurants, laundries.

Came Coca Cola, Levis Jeans. Came iPod.

And somewhere in this story of faith
the hill of hell was made heaven
in the name of Francis.

V.

From the arched window of the public toilet
in the Basilica atop Assisi, wash your hands,
stand at the window high above the Umbrian Plain
and that distant cathedral encasing the chapel
is centered in the window—buildings, streets,
trees, fields, clouds, arranged the way a photographer
arranges her world a frame at a time,
or the artist who frescoed the people of the Bible
until they breathed in the mind,
almost talked to the illiterate a chapter at a time,
so that if you accosted a village boy,
or the gray haired *nonna* attending the toilet,
saying, "San Pietro is only a story; he never lived;
he never died." Either would take you, saying, *andiamo*,
into the basilica, the back altar, right arm of Jesus,

and point to the fading cross painted
upside down on the wall,
whisper the saint's name,
and shake a finger at

you.

VI.

Because we honor the years of our love,
we fly to Rome then bus to seven cities in twelve days.
On the sixth day we stand in line to touch
the wooden feet of Jesus on the cross
at the altar in the chapel Francis built.

I do not ask if you felt how sharp
was the point of the nail sticking through,
or if you noticed how bright were the eyes
of the young Brother at the exit
whose palm was extended for offerings.
Or if you offered.

Who knows why his eyes glowed?
Praying to the Saint?
Contemplating the white striped feather by his sandal?
The glitter of coins, though not his own, weighing his hand?

When we came out of that chapel,
no washed sky or sun drenched clouds greeted us.
Instead, the frescos, marble and stained glass windows
of the cathedral arched overhead, stone above stone,
so much hardness interceding between the heaven

of Francis dying
and waking to new life.

We circled the chapel,
bowed our heads in the muted light,
walked out a door tall as trees
where wind bent branches and shoved the clouds aside.

VII.

        i.

Doves become pigeons, noisy, jealous, usurping all
the places the public lounges on days off,
whether Central Park or Piazza San Marco, Venezia—
Look at the fools trying to befriend
those ugly things, childish dreams of talking to the birds.
The children know. Watch them in
Trafalgar Square, Jardin de Luxembourg, Marienplatz—
kicking at those unclean birds.

Greed and murder the bouquets we give the other.
Tell me again, Sir, why it is God's will for fathers
to strap bombs to their daughters?
Is not a daughter more
than the nothingness of the foul air
after the blast?
Did you not see in her
as she worked her school lessons
a paradise the grandfathers spoke of?
Will she not, however she manages, extend the family
and thereby add to the blood's wealth?
If you kill your daughters, who will kneel and weep
at your draped coffin?

Greed and peace—oil and water spreading
across the world today.

If you talk to animals they lock you up.
If you march for peace surveillance cameras
catalogue your every movement like a wolf stalking.
Someone puts your name and photo in a computer.

It is not good. *In nomini Patre...*
a failed policy.

A small hope when John XXIII proclaimed one feast day for Saint Francis: "Whoever has more abundant wealth must give more generously, giving also for those who are unable to do so. The precept applies not only to two brothers, two families or two towns, but to the whole world."

They took this John, embalmed him,
sealed him in a glass coffin,
like Lenin in that wall,
and put the coffin behind the altar of St. Peter's,
where every day people parade past
that beaked nose, those pointed slippers,
the dreamer's promise, the fisherman's promise, *et al.*

They snap a picture,
walk out under the cruel sun of Piazza San Pietro
and never return.

Oil and water . . .

It is not good . . .

                    ii.

If you decry the sun's architecture
your days will be cloudy, the heart moonless

If you welcome the giant of nothing into your home
trees will weep fruit that will not feed even the birds

If you rage into the night
divorce will steal all the tomorrows

If you accept death before you live
your dogs will be unmanageable, your children angry

Be cautious of spider lace in the windows—
it is not charity

If you hear nothing
the ruin is within

If you believe only a radiant woman can save you
then you may walk once again beneath stars

Because the grass greens each spring
and dandelions crown the meadow

and apple trees blossom
death is only metaphor

Someone is speaking from far away
he says, *Death will breed in the gardens of poets*

iii.

Because the beggar woman by Bernini's fountain in Rome's
Piazza Navona, the one with the lion in the cave of water,
showed me her infant's deformed legs, then smiled and lifted
her face to me when I placed a euro in her hand, then bowed
her head, but I had seen in her dark eyes a light that said,
*"Truly I am not that old, and that once I was beautiful and still
carry the memory of that beauty ..."*

Because a man in story long ago rejected wealth and fashion
walked when he could have ridden
recognized spirit in nature and followed it
translated birdsong as prayer

Because a child ignores the tourists and only steps
on the white stones to enter the cathedral

Because sheep graze the hillside

Because a woman loves you

there is God

There

is

.

IV.

A PARIS CHRISTMAS

Was it all just the air of that hotel room,
antiqued with the traffic of countless couples
who fled night under frayed sheets?

The gray light of Christmas day
leaked through mist to pierce
the glassed balcony doors and settled

about your face like a veil. Time ceased
progression and for this moment
you were a too-human Madonna,

childless, sitting on the bed, the breakfast
bread crumbling down shoulders, breasts, and lap.
I sat cradled in the worn chair facing you,

straining the dimmed light into focus and still
couldn't see what needed seeing. We dressed
then roamed a nameless garden, light rain filling

the honeymoon silences, the coy smiles.
Now more than anything, I remember those bright
crumbs sparkling on your winter pale skin

like the gold offered by a foolish magi.

THE BEAUTIFUL LANGUAGE

She sits again on a bench along the canal
in Rotterdam, waiting. This is where
he will come, she whispers to herself.
She feels him stirring under her bones.
Behind her the Euromast rises, swaying
gently in the permanent breeze,
its tiered café full of quiet activity.

         Tourists
smile at the demitasses and the scenery,
both grateful and awed to be here. Even
their children are subdued with this now
in their lives, this moment they will not
remember as adults. Lovers gaze into
their narrowing eyes, knees kissing beneath
the small tables. They could be anywhere
in the world and that place would still
be heightened by their inflamed blood.
On the roof a young American and his
bride marvel at these vast lowlands
that are someone else's lives.

         On the bench
a woman waits for the angel who appeared
in her dream. His silver eyes glowed with
rapture. He drifted by in a boat on the air.
She doesn't know if he will greet her
in Dutch or French, or some language
known only in the soul. Her heart
is ready.

    The young couple high above her
sway in the wind washed air and embrace
in the only beautiful language possible
between flesh and flesh.

GRAVITY LIKES YOU GOING DOWN

A girl looks out her bedroom window
in the farmhouse her great-grandfather
built and smiles at the new day
as you remember the shooting star last night,
how its explosive kiss lit the darkness.

You pretend to look out the portal of the airplane
circling above Amsterdam. You've heard of its sudden fall
to the next hold, and the next,
a forty minute descent before the wheels
touch on Dutch asphalt,
not far from where Brueghel imagined Icarus falling.

You buy the train pass, a sandwich, bottle of beer.
At the Bahnhof in Cologne a man asks you
to pose for photographs.
He promises *vielgeld*. He follows you
to the stairs of the cathedral, does not enter.
Inside you walk to the middle pew,
sit, pray silently
until you notice the light through the stained glass
shines all around, but doesn't touch you.

A lederhosened hiker stepped down
from the Alpenweg beneath Bischofsmütze,
down to the *hostelerei* where you meet,
and fall further in dream.

In Belgrade a despot's idol to himself
is hauled down among gun shots—
the revolutionaries' cheers will not last; they, too,
will swirl in the dust circling your torn sneakers.

When you don't give alms to the beggar boy
in Istanbul, he steals your shoulder bag
and runs down the smokey alley
across from the Blue Mosque shouting,
Teseqir...Teseqir. After a week of the embassy's
charity, of the ambassador's third assistant taking you

to a hotel room each afternoon,
you have a new passport and a ticket home.
When you leave, the young Marine guard,
all spit-shined and once hopeful, no longer smiles at you.

Even though a dog leaps in London's Hyde Park
to snatch a frisbee from flight,
the police photographer's angle makes the dog leap
above your torn body crumpled on the grass.
You see the photo on the front page
of tomorrow's *Mirror*. You want to cry.
Readers will call the city editor to say
My daughter left home last month; is this poor girl her?

But you've been watching a dahlia
in the garden by the barn, its withered face droops
closer to the mulch, closer until it falls.
Your little sister picks up the wasted flower,
pulls a few petals, grows disgusted with red goo
on her fingers, throws it down, walks away
with a rusting wagon in tow.

That night you wait for sleep. When it arrives,
the dream is the same. You won't see
how your lips turn down.

OBERAMMERGAU

Eight thousand citizens live one dream
and keep the same passionate promise

inherited from hundreds of years of farmers
and woodcarvers, of bankers and waiters

and shop keepers, who paint their homes,
restaurants and hotels, wear lederhosen

and village dirndl dresses, hang geraniums
from every window, because God likes

tradition and beauty, because tourists
spend dollars and marks and kronin

for quaintness and covenant, because
eight thousand know what is not lost.

SWIMMING WITH THE SWANS

Zell am See, Austria

i.

When three swans float near,
a crowd gathers

and those with children
teach them what is beautiful.

The swans tilt and turn their heads
expecting handouts.

When no one tosses
stale bread into the water,

the swans drift to other people
further down the shore,

because their beauty,
by itself,

is cause enough
for gifts.

ii.

Four swans two dozen yards from shore
glide on the water in this glacial lake.

When they turn to face the rising sun,
a man's head appears among them,

swimming in the European manner,
wakeless, nearly soundless,

which allowed him, in the first place,
to swim with the swans. The man

seems torn between water and air,
wishing either gills or feathers adorn

his simple flesh. He dips beneath
the water, surfaces as the swans drift

beyond his reach. He paddles back
to shore, stands in dry air, and walks

to the bathhouse, neck and head
high and full of grace.

CABLE CAR RIDE

Kitzbuehel, Austria

Six of us climb into the red cable car
with one desire: the height of gods.

We swing, we sway on wire
that seems too thin but isn't.

We joke about accidents, about what
our bodies would look like

crushed below. When we step
from the car we sigh then laugh.

The air atop an Alpine mountain
in August thrills more than lungs.

Each deep breath brings us closer
to the makers of this world

spread below us like a board game—
put a village here, a trolley car there,

push the rain to a farther valley,
have geese alight on this lake.

We watch the white clouds kiss
the next peak and grow jealous

we are not over there,
hugged by heaven like the angels.

THE ECONOMICS OF RAIN

1995

There are no trees on the streets
of Sarajevo. The parks are wastelands
of grass trampled to mud,
where litter, tree-stump holes
and craters decorate the eye's path.
Children wander, seeking those
little somethings, a dropped board,
a fat branch, a lost water bottle
to carry home, to make a mother smile.
Winter is coming. It rains.
One cold more the world expectorates,
like spitting on your own shoe.
They chopped down the last tree
within the city limits this past winter;
its naked beauty forsaken for fuel.
The fierce rain blackens the cements walls
of Olympic Village Apartments
wherein a girl says to her widowed
mother, "I wish it would stop raining."
Mother nods, knowing snow
is next, and whispers,
"We have paid, but the price changes."
She hums to barter with night.

BEETHOVEN IN THE RAIN

i. Plaudite

Such an old man alone on the streets in the rain in Vienna,
such a squat, old man with greatcoat to the ankles,
with haggard boots shattering puddles like chandelier fugues
while splashing and soaking the hem of disregard
for fashion in clothing, emperor, or music,
such an old man alone ignoring each new step along the
        Danubeweg
because Napoleon rears his horse toward Austria,
because the body of Haydn rots in the soaked and silent ground,
because there is no other substance than pure sound,
such an old man walking with eyes beyond the rain,
with ears as useful as the blind moon above the rain,
such an old man shuffling through water drawn cobblestone
without the patience of stone, without water's direction, but
        ablaze with its gravity,
an old man without patron or position walking through
        destiny's sodden fog,
who crosses the city square to be named Mozartplatz,
who passes in forlornness the rollicking concert halls,
who snubs each ghost that sang to the velvet seats,
or played there some sacred echo, or kept a score clogged with
        baton,
because the last scribblings at the piano are always bruised,
because the past makes less sense than the unscripted music
        sounding beyond the reverie of dream,
beyond what rises again in the hollows of the chest to
        command the soul
to seize each note and drench it in beauty,
such a man walking in the rain.

ii. amici

You acknowledge no one
        in these walks.
You speak to no one
        in a loud, gruff voice
                driven by deafness
                        and mania.
You might as well be
        talking
                to angels
afterall
        everyone called you
                The Crazed Genius
                        though not to your face.

Even neighbors
        who pass you
                on the street,
                        see your hands
                                gesticulating
                                        to no one,

(tell the truth, old man:
        you were conducting
            a symphony
                    of rain!)

the neighbors
        become
                alarmed and
                        hasten on
                                down the soppy
                                        streets of Vienna.

iii. comoedia finita est

Old Ludwig, alone in the rain, accompanied
by apparitions of childhood: The soggy father
and sloppy mother who lowered herself for a husband.

Old Ludwig, drinking the rain of remembrance,
what hat could corral that large head and surf of hair about
       to crash,
a finale as grand as anything imagined in deafness?

Old Louis so arduous and alone in that rain:
Is it true you fell in love with every woman you met?
Nicht war? Sie haben alles geliebt?

Helena und Elise,
Johanna und Maria Magdalena,
Bettina und Sophia,

Anna Maria und Dorothea,
Princess Marie und Toni,
O Immortal Beloved,

O Geliebte!

O Louis!

iv. Schade, schade—zu spät

O Freude, O Joy—What does it matter
that it rains in Vienna
when adagios clear the air!
What does it matter that tyrants rule the body

when air and rain are free,
when violins and pianos and cellos
are their own law
and speak the only truth worth imagining.

There is a sketch of you walking in the rain:
Tall hat weeping, large, ill-fitted coat
hanging from down cast shoulders,
collar upright, tight to the back of the neck,

eyes staring at nothing visible,
mouth angled and angry, preoccupied
with whatever it was
you sifted from the deaf air.

Your death bed drawing repeated in books
could frighten children into behaving.
But the sketch of you in the rain
would scare angels. So what

if its original is lost. So much leaches down
the drains. At least the friends standing
watch by your sick bed recorded
the last words you spoke for posterity:

Applaud, friends, the comedy is ended.

Then just before the coma
they told you
the wines from Mainz finally arrived
and you whispered, *Pity, pity—too late.*

And the echo,

Pity, pity—too late / Schade, schade—zu spät
Pity— too late / Schade— zu spät
Pity, pity / Schade, schade
too late / zu spät
late / spät
late

THE DAY BEFORE HER 50TH BIRTHDAY

In the Cathedral of Salzburg,
amid the gilt and cornished plaster,
beneath Mozart's organ restored after the war,
we pray for my newly dead
father and mother,
who made babies, worked and died
in the city of their birth,
who never traveled
except in magazines and television,
except for the war in the Pacific,
except mother, late in life,
with her only daughter,
taking bus tours to Graceland and Branson
as cancer cells bloomed
in her blood,
and we pray for your father,
a few years dead,
your father, here in Austria
as guest of the German government
during the war,
who met a girl from his homeland,
also a guest,
in the work camp near Graz,
whom he married after liberation,
when, for the first time in years,
he was free to be a man
in the true sense,
not the one defined by a rifle in hand,
but with a woman
in his arms,
and a baby, you,
in his arms, in Leoben,
and we whisper a last little prayer
for ourselves,
our long loving,
in the still air
of this thousand year old
vault of prayers,
where, before we leave,
we light three candles.

A FULL MOON IN SWITZERLAND

The Alps alter all perspective.
From the balcony of Hotel Bruening
in Hergiswil near Luzern, the full

August moon rises at the same angle
Mt. Pilatus slopes its black bulk
to the lake whose dark water

ripples and dims the light reflected
as the moon struggles to lift
above the line of rock and gravity.

I wonder how deep into the deep lake
the moon's light knifes, if salmon
huddle in those depths to ward off

this monthly terror. I wonder that
this same moon's light earlier shone
on the fragments of bodies

at the embassy bombed in Nairobi,
or on the wet cheeks of the families
of the dead gathered to mourn.

The lights of a fisherman's boat
glide to the dock with barely a sound.
I wonder if he caught the big one.

Ninety degree heat and humidity
in these mountains. The world changing
right before our eyes. Old people

dying. Governments struck dumb.
I suck ice on this balcony this August
waiting for a breeze and wonder

how many other people use this time
to contemplate this moon pushing
through their own small square of night.

AGE 23 WORDSWORTH SLEEPS IN STONEHENGE

After days tramping the Salisbury Plains,
he crept to the center of that stone puzzle,
the point of honor in an antique calendar
of the unknown, and lay himself down
on soft grass to sleep.

The dance of diurnal starlight ignored,
the moon's form deranged, the ghosts
of hooded men silent in an obsolete universe,
he joined the slow dream of stone.

He awoke to morning washing his lips,
to war exploding beyond the circle, to young men
lured by a cheap shilling into a slavish Navy,
to widows starving. And that distant voice
closing in was the world, that became his song.

EMERSON AT GRASMERE

Roused from a noontide nap, Wordsworth
didn't know his guest, didn't
recognize him, didn't remember him
from the visit thirteen years before.
So many came to pay homage,
to have a story to tell, to say, "I sat
by the fire with Mr Wordsworth
and we talked about the trains' ruination
of the country side," or "Wordsworth and I
walked his garden and he recited to me
a sonnet about mountains and lakes
and village girls,…" which is exactly
what Emerson seized during his first visit
and said the poems were the loveliest
he'd ever heard, but wrote that the white
haired poet was *disfigured by green goggles*,
that he talked with *great simplicity*, and
was taken aback by *the hard limits of his
thought*. Shocking from so honored a man.
But what could any loyal subject of the king
expect from an American renegade, fresh
from rejecting his ministry and about
to recast the American Dream.
So the sleep denied poet rambled on,
disjointed, confused, insecure, with
death, as unstoppable as ever, less
than a year away. Mr. Emerson left,
certain his earlier conception of this man,
now *a bitter old Englishman*, was true.

OSCAR WILDE BRINGS FLOWERS TO HIS WIFE'S GRAVE

The sea had no sparkle on Oscar Wilde's
last trip to Genoa, and the sun hesitated
over the greedy horizon. First lunch, tasteless,

mechanical, the wine even worse. Then
the cemetery. He lingered before a marble cross
and touched his wife's carved name.

He carried flowers.
What else could he bring her in death
that he hadn't in life.

The surrounding hills soft, delicate,
a token of early spring.
The shock of her name divorced from his:

> Constance Mary
> daughter of
> Horace Lloyd

as if Oscar never was, marriage a sham,
mere convention to a phobic public. Yet here
he stood in the garden of her resting,

muttering to himself, *the uselessness
of regret*. He wasn't thinking about
the money problems her death

would cause; that came later,
when he wrote, *sunlight is half
my income*. He didn't think about

his sons in London he'd never see again.
He placed the flowers by the stone
and prayed she knew he loved her also.

ANOTHER MIRACLE IN THE ENGLISH CHANNEL

If the sea parts before you
and you can now walk

straight from Dover to Calais,
take this small blessing.

No life is at stake. No genocide.
Just a free revelation of the ocean's floor.

No *Titanics* broken
and half-swallowed in muck.

All the fish will be gone.
A few mollusks, perhaps, maybe

a lobster, gasping, waving
antennae in the senseless air.

Take off your shoes. Roll up your pants.
Whistle, if you will, and be wary of sea birds

who may be so confused they drop
at your feet, no longer capable of flight.

Do not be surprised if dozens of them
fall in line behind you. Think of it, man,

you, with gulls, terns, and plovers,
walking and rehearsing *Bonjour*.

DAUGHTER OF ALEXANDRIA

The tri-colored cats of Rome,
half tame, lounged on the sun
drenched stone steps of the Colosseum,
hind feet dangling over the edge.
They were everywhere, waiting for
hand outs. We walked past them and stood
at the top looking down, at the whole
ruined structure and how it seemed to curve
its walls toward us like arms in a hug.
I've been dreaming those cats,
wondering if they are the children
of Cleopatra. She climbed these steps,
probably with feet as delicate as yours.
Caesar brought her here but forgot
the trouble she was to her people,
spawning widows crying the nights
empty for years. Even the gods
were helpless against such wailing.
Can you picture Cleopatra at your age,
tinting strands of gray from her hair,
yet holding the breath of dark youth?
She was Greek, a daughter of Alexandria.
Sometimes I dream you are Greek,
that I stole you from a mountain village,
that decades later your brothers
and their sons hunt me still. I saw
them staring behind glass as we boarded
airplanes, a step ahead of them again.
When that customs inspector pulled you
aside at Heathrow, I knew he wasn't
English, eyes too dark, too deep.
I was ready to abandon luggage, grab
your hand and run along corridors,
down stairwells, through secret
passageways to jump the train, but he
only asked if you were really American,
then accepted your assurances, even
though you aren't. He saw in you
the Cleopatra I did that day

we explored the walls and tunnels
of the ruined Roman baths in Trier,
stumbled out of the darkness into
the open courtyard just as the gray
German sky gave way to sun and its light
draped your shoulders. You glowed
like all the women Botticelli painted.
That was when you showed her
to me. That was when you were
twenty and my bride.

WHEN I SAW THE WILD RABBIT

When I saw the wild rabbit licking
seeds off the February ground beneath
the bird feeder, dark tongue impervious
to all but its need, I didn't think of
the struggle life can be. Instead, I saw us
years ago in the shower of a Salzburg hotel
as you turned off the spray and we stood
in that small enclosure, dripping and gleaming,
your tongue licking the wet from my shoulder,
impervious to all but our love.

BORN IN WATER

In a small lake in the North of Ireland
sits Church Island, rock and spruce.
If you look hard enough, you might see
a small, dark globe shining between
green branches that shape a spire.
It is a sea eagle's eye. It is sated,
having clawed a salmon just
as early mist lifted. It will not stir
until sunrise. But you have probably
been distracted by the two boys
splashing in that deep, cold water.
Haying done, they dropped clothes
on the mossy bank and dove in
so readily you know it's not
the first time they wash the dust of hay
from hair, nose, throat. One boy dives
to fool the other. But it's different
this time. Down there he hears
a waterborne echo, a song
like a prayer, its rhythm
as slow as granite molting.
By now the other boy has climbed
the shore, dressed, and stands
worrying the solid earth. He shouts,
"Seamus. Seamus. This is no kind joke!"
The boy, in an envelope of water,
sang as in dream, until a pain
in the lungs calls him to look
where the white hole of sky recedes.
He gives a firm kick and pulls himself up.
Splashing and gasping, he shouts,
"Tommy...I heard them...Voices.
Like mermaids...Like angels!"
Thomas would have none of it.
He hauls his friend ashore,
admonishes him. The boy dresses
in silence. The air tastes different
to him, new. He will spend
his days dreaming the voices.

ACKNOWLEDGMENTS

Amelia: "Briseis in Midtown"
Asphodel: "Leonardo"
Bloodroot Literary Magazine: "Daughter of Alexandria"
Buckle &: "The Colosseum"
Crying Sky: "Villa Pomphili Park"
Diner: "Belly Dancer"
Evening Street Review: "#4729 Silver Diadem with Dentilated
       Border"
5 AM: "A Kiss Behind The Campidoglio" (under the title:
       "The Campidoglio"), "Stealing Troy iii."
Front Range Review: "The Butcher"
Gargoyle: "Age 23 Wordsworth Sleeps in Stonehenge"
Glacial Hills Review: "Stealing Troy ii."
Heavy Bear: "History as Hobby"
Hawai'i Pacific Review: "Saint Matthew in the Stone"
Ibbetson Street: "Stealing Troy i.," "After the Revelation," "The
       Flesh in Marble" (under the title "Fragmentary Story
       of the Flesh in Marble") and "Oscar Wilde Brings
       Flowers to His Wife's Grave"
Iodine Poetry Journal: "Oberammergau"
Istanbul Literary Review (Turkey): "In Three Languages,"
       "The Economics of Rain," "Gravity Likes You Going
       Down"
Misfit Magazine: "In the Sistine Chapel: i. Inventing secret
       signs"
Nixes Mate Review and *Nixes Mate Review Anthology*: "How
       the Conquerors Settled"
oyez review: "Another Miracle in the English Channel"
Perigee: "In the Sistine Chapel: iii. If God hath a beard"
Poetry East: "Peace," "Outside the Keats-Shelley House," "The
       Room of Faces"
PoetryMagazine.com: "A Full Moon in Switzerland," "Making
       Love in Athens"
Poetry Salzburg Review (Austria): "The Bridge of Sighs"

riverrun: "Cable Car Ride"
Rushing Thru the Dark: "Stealing Troy iv."
Snake Nation Review: "The Day Before Her 50th Birthday"
Stone Country: "Smyrna"
Tears in the Fence (UK): "Beethoven in the Rain"
Tar Wolf Review: "Juliet on the Balcony"
The Alembic: "Swimming with the Swans ii."
The Country and Abroad: "Ruins"
The Pedestal Magazine: "Born in Water"
Wilderness House Literary Review: "Beneath the Blue Realm"
VerseWrights: "The Anonymous Closet," "The Beautiful
         Language"
Your Daily Poem.com: "One Day in the Apennines"
"Francis d'Assisi 2008"chapbook, Finishing Line Press, 2008

ABOUT THE AUTHOR

Gary Metras was appointed the inaugural Poet Laureate of the City of Easthampton in 2018. His essays, reviews, and chiefly poems have appeared in hundreds of journals since the 1970s, including *America, American Angler, Boston Review of Books, The Common, Connecticut Poetry Review, Gray's Sporting Journal, Poetry, Poetry East, Salzburg Poetry Review,* and *Yankee Magazine*. He has taught high school English and college writing. A master letterpress printer, he ran Adastra Press for forty years, publishing poets from all over the country.

www.ingramcontent.com/pod-product-compliance
Lightning Source LLC
Chambersburg PA
CBHW021343090426
42742CB00008B/716